Julian
of Norwich's
Teabag

Julian of Norwich's Teabag

Poems and prayers from morning to night

Martin Wroe

wild goose
publications

www.**ionabooks**.com

First published 2022 by
Wild Goose Publications
Suite 9, Fairfield
1048 Govan Road, Glasgow G51 4XS, Scotland
the publishing division of the Iona Community.
Scottish Charity No. SC003794. Limited Company Reg. No. SC096243.

ISBN 978-1-80432-253-6

Cover image © Meg Wroe

Overseas distribution
Australia: Willow Connection Pty Ltd, 1/13 Kell Mather Drive,
Lennox Head NSW 2478
New Zealand: Pleroma, Higginson Street, Otane 4170,
Central Hawkes Bay

Printed in the UK by Page Bros (Norwich) Ltd

CONTENTS

Evening

Night

For Meg
the poem I find life with

This perforated planet

In the Venn diagram where the circles of poetry, prayer and psalm overlap, there's a sweet spot.

If you wanted to mark this spot, you might call it 'heaven in ordinary', an overlooked place where a found poem finds that, at any moment in a day, the numinous is hiding in plain sight.

This collection of poems is in search of that location, the place on the day's map where a poem may be disguised as a prayer, a psalm as a song lyric.

These are not poems for transcendent times, for the hour when you first believed or the place where the two roads diverged in the yellow wood and you took the one less travelled because, well, you had to take one of them.

These are poems found in ordinary days, the ones we don't think twice about and yet, in the act of paying attention, discover that every living moment holds a hunch that it contains more than itself.

Watching the light bursting through the curtains first thing in the morning, trying to stay awake on a Zoom call or following your clothes as they rotate in the launderette.

These are poems found as the first cup of tea brews and the recycling lorry trundles down the street; as the children grow up and someone you love dies; as we rage against life and as love brings us home.

These are lines which try to see the world through the same spectacles as the 14th-century mystic Julian of Norwich. Some were written during two months volunteering on Iona, where Columba washed up from Ireland eight centuries before Julian.

If those two started a band, I'd want to play in it.

'It is all that is made.' That's Julian, in Norwich
Tripping on a hazelnut in her 14th-century grip
My trip is this teabag, giving up its love
This perforated planet, in my steaming mug

Martin Wroe

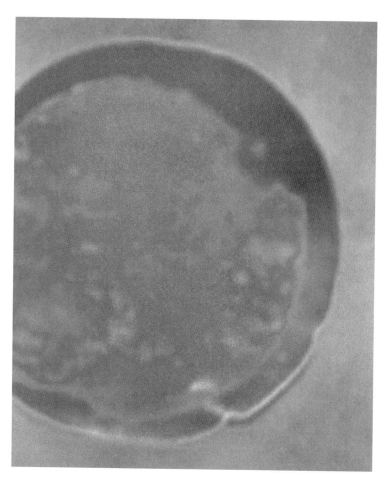

MORNING

Here comes the day

Here comes the day,
Goodness and badness
Light in our dark,
Joy in our sadness
We clamber aboard
We take in the view
When it all feels impossible
When it all feels untrue
We love one another
That's all we can do

Wake-up call

To whom it may concern
A brief note of gratitude
For the wake-up call of life
The morning's bright beatitude

For the altos and sopranos
The birdsong in the trees
For this symphonic canopy
The choir that shakes the leaves

For this book of common prayer
That's winging through the air
For the melody of first light
That sings good day to night

Curtain

Through a gap
In the curtain
The light arrives
Eight minutes
Twenty seconds
Ninety-three million miles

From the sun
To my window
I open my eyes
All this way
To bring us a day
Better try and do it right

Front door

It's 7.49am.
You've just gone out the front door.
You pulled it hard, to catch the lock.
It didn't catch, so I walked towards it
To give it a push.
As I reached out to push
You reached back, to give it a pull.
I saw you through the stained glass,
Reaching back, even as you were leaving.
You pulled it shut
Before I got there. I smiled.
You were gone.

I'll always be reaching for the door
That you've gone through.
I know you have to leave,
But I'll always be hoping you might return.
I'll always be looking for you,
As the years stain and blur.
One day you won't stop and turn.
You won't reach back.
But I'll always be at the door
Just in case.
It's 7.59am.

Dawn from on high

The dawn from on high
Breaks upon us again
Unplugging the night
Connecting the day
A tender compassion
Angelic satellite
We sit in the darkness
With a promise of sight

Give us this day

Give us this day
Our daily bread
Peace in our hearts
Calm in our heads
Give us this day
Whatever the struggle
Peace in our world
Whatever the trouble
Give us all faith
In each other

Open

Let me hold
A door open
Invite someone in
Let someone pass
Point out a way
Pass them a key

Let me hold
The door open
That was opened
For me

Surprise us

At the beginning of a day
The idea is that you will
Walk with us
And we will try
To walk with you
We already know we will
Forget you
In a moment
Not notice you
Then ignore you
Forget we were here
At the beginning of the day
Asking you to be with us

                                        … but our

Intentions are good
So …
                                        … surprise us

In the face of friend
Or stranger
Wink at us from a dilemma
Or frown from an argument
Catch our eye from laptop or mobile
                              … but don't forget us
The way we're about to forget you
Pursue us
Even as we
Run from you

Chase us
Catch us
Trip us
Overtake us
Hide behind the unexpected
And
Leap
Out in front

                                        … and remind us

Of these good intentions
To walk with you
At the beginning of the day
And find you
Walking with us
Till its end

Apocalypse

The recycling lorry
Canters down the road
Delaying the arrival
Of the Four Horsemen
Of the Apocalypse

Morning has broken

Morning has broken
But afternoon
Has not yet spoken
Although the day
Seems to be getting away
Maybe the evening will have
Something to say

True north

Be the compass
In my hand this day
Pointing true north,
Showing the way
Be the company
At my side this day
Walk with me
All the way

Morning

'Morning'
He looks up at me, astonished
'Morning'
Disturbed, surprised, briefly baffled
'Morning'
A smile, a courtesy, a nod of the head
'Morning'
One word plus eye contact
A small act of resistance
Against the anonymity of our urban village
'Morning'
Two women look at me, then at each other,
Then giggling as I pass
'Morning'
His expression is making a calculation of me:
'Is this man getting the help he needs?'
'Morning'
I smile and look openly at each one I pass
But sometimes I read a thought in their startled eyes
– in that nano-second before they avert them –
'How far is it to safety?'

'Morning'
It started when I recognised someone on the canal path
'Morning'
I said, before realising, as he replied, uncertainly,
'Morning'
– looking at me with a face that said, 'we've never met' –
That recognising someone is not knowing them
And that I recognised his face only from his picture byline

In *The Guardian* newspaper, which was the building
I'd just walked past
And he was walking towards
Doubtless already wondering
If I could be worked into the opening of a column
About mental health and urban deprivation.

'Morning'
I said to the next person,
As they jumped physically from the world inside their phone
'Morning'
I was starting to feel defiant
Why shouldn't we greet each other
Just because we don't know each other?
'Morning'
I changed the ringtone slightly,
Going up a note on the second syllable
*'Mor-**ning**'*
Next time down on the first
*'**Mor**-ning'*
To see if I could draw someone's gaze
From inside their universe and into mine
'Morning'
I didn't want to alarm anyone
Better to let them see it was me, with the greeting
A tall, bespectacled, middle-aged man,
Albeit smiling toward them,
Weirdly – they might think –
'Morning'
The man from *The Guardian* had
Reminded me of the night I met a famous woman
In The Coronet on Holloway Road

She was standing by me at the bar
A household name in a household I couldn't place
As I studied her from my side eye
Googling my memory to establish her celebrity credentials
Scanning the image files of my internal film and TV database
– Who is she? What's she been in? –
She glanced back at me,
As if she also knew me.
Or maybe it was just a funny look.
Only when I took everyone's drinks back to the table,
Did it dawn on me:
Of course
She's another of those people I don't know but *do* know
Although her fame is limited and fairly local.
That's how I know her,
From the checkout, at Waitrose.

We know each other and we don't, I thought
– now back on the towpath – connected
To those we think we're not
Maybe that's why I said
'Morning'
To the next person on the towpath
An invisible insurrection
In favour of connection
'Morning'
This man is surprised, but also, looks sort of grateful
'Alright mate, how you doing?'
'Great, thanks, have a good one …'
'Morning'

A smile, a courtesy, a nod of the head
'Morning'
'Hey! How are you?'
We're now on the Cally Road.
'Haven't seen you in ages'
Thirty-something, casually dressed, wide-eyed, enquiring
'Are you still playing?' he asks,
Appearing to know me
I stand there, smiling back,
Wondering how to play it
'Actually,' I say, 'I don't think we've met'
But, honestly, I'm having my doubts
'It's *me*,' he says, as if I don't know he's *him*
'Football,' he says, 'I haven't played for ages'
'No, sorry,' I say, 'I think you've mistaken me
I was just saying *Morning* because …'

My words trail off, no need to explain
It's all in the eyes
He's looking at me
I'm looking at him
We get that we don't know each other
And also that next time we meet
We'll know that we do
Even as we remember
That we don't.

Today is World Day For Being Today

Today is World Day For Being Today
Today has not been sponsored or underwritten
Today is not coming to you on behalf of anything
Except itself
Today is not looking for a partnership
Except one with you
Today is not looking for promotion
Or a corporate identity
And will not be selling off the rights to
This afternoon or this evening
Although
Later
Today will rebrand itself as
Tomorrow
But until then
Today is fine
Thanks

Today is already a good cause
Like every day
Today is OK

A blessing for a meeting on Zoom

In the place where eye contact is impossible
The silent lexicon of non-verbal cues extinct
May this not be the crowd without the wisdom
Despite our isolation, our social distance

May we give thanks for this awkward digital blessing
May we be admitted, May we not be muted
May our distorted sound and scrambled words
Finally align, May they catch up with our pixelated vision
May travelling this unfamiliar landscape
Neither lose us, nor exhaust us
And may our bandwidth always find room
For patience, gentleness and the peace
That bypasses misunderstanding.

May every meeting open and close with a poem,
A joke or a steadying moment of silence
Some brief transfiguration in time, to remind us
Of who we were, before all this,
And who we may be again
May our agenda always be kindness
The waving hand, our ecstatic benediction
And may there never be any other business
For ever and ever. Amen

Grounded

If this day is grounded
Refuses to take off
If it runs out of fuel
Comes to a full stop
Remind me of days which rise
On wings like eagles
When we run and we run
And do not grow weary

I lift up my eyes (lockdown psalm)

I lift up my eyes from this lockdown
Outside, I cover my face
My friends become danger
I become threat, I step aside,
As you pass

Inside, these walls close in,
This safety and this cage
Inside, we're too close
And, a little distant
Inside, I'm alone, I'm scared
I lift up my eyes from this lockdown

I lift up my eyes,
They are wet from my tears
My days slip through these bone-dry fingers
From where will my help come
To carry me, or hold me,
With faith, hope and love?

My help comes in a window box
The shy defiance of a daffodil
On the street, the conversation of the trees
The dance of every season,
The dawn, the dusk
How they carry us

My help comes inside PPE,
From those who care and those who heal,
And a friend who calls, across the way,
Can you believe this? How's your day?

My help comes from those who sit and listen
When I no longer make sense
Who wash me clean, and break a broken blessing over me
Who walk beside us when we die
They neither slumber nor sleep
How they carry us

My help comes in those who love me
I hold them tenderly, in all this silence,
That cradles all the sorrow, all the loss
All this love in all this life
How this carries us

I hold them all, they hold me
Wherever I go, they go with me
At my going out and my coming in,
Even when I cannot catch another breath
Still, they breathe my life

I lift up my eyes and see
That Love will keep our lives,
From this time forth, for evermore.

From the first hello

From the first hello
To the last goodbye
Looking for the friend
In the stranger's eye
The smallest talk
The heart-to-heart
The grammar of signs
Unspoken thoughts
The gift of attention
The keeping quiet
Looking for each other
Every day of our lives

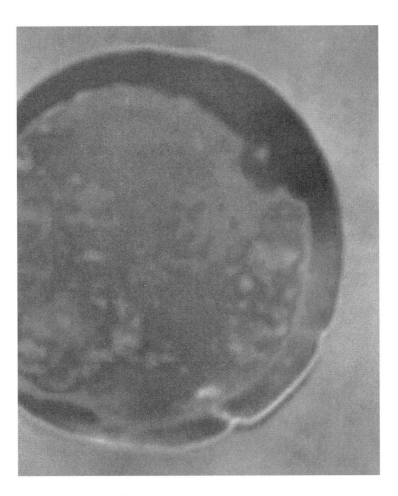

AFTERNOON

Julian of Norwich's teabag

'It is all that is made.' That's Julian, in Norwich
Tripping on a hazelnut in her 14th-century grip
My trip is this teabag, giving up its love
This perforated planet, in my steaming mug

Onward flight in the dark of compost bin,
With potato peel, onion and banana skin
From Sri Lanka or Kenya, this leafy supernova
Here in my kitchen, this miraculous stopover

The quiet humus of mineralisation
Organic breakdown, mostly just waiting
How earth flavours and fires this life every day
I get it, Julian, this teabag, how it's all that is made

Light

Set your light
On my path
When the day
Goes very dark
Set some star
In the sky
Walk with me
At my side

For what we are about to receive

For what we are about to receive
The water we drink
The air we breathe
The fire of sun
The food of earth
This company, these people
This now, this here,
May we be thankful
May we be aware
How every day is a gift
And every breath a prayer

The meeting

It was a meeting
That's all. Just another

Time and place where we all
Got together. It wasn't a party

No clinking glasses,
Anecdote and laughter

No-one had been looking
Forward to it for ages

The minutes of the previous one
Felt like hours. I wondered what the agenda

Was hiding. I didn't know it was this
Subtle revolution. None of us knew

But that was how it all started, when
The future showed up under any other business

Inviting us over to her place, asking us if we'd
Ever had this thought, the one she'd just given us.

Thinking back, we were in some kind of
Laboratory, not knowing what this experiment

Would lead to, as if we had a chemistry
None of us had guessed at

Hit reset

Slow. Stop.
Take a deep breath
Stand stock still.
Hit reset.
Here is the day
Cherish the sight.
Notice your life
As it's passing by.

The gate

The gate comes back to me, unannounced
Hanging there, a frame which frames itself.
Sitting high on a trailer of hay bales
I'm looking backward across the shorn field
Mr Benfield, at the wheel of the tractor
Pulling us roughly along, and, at first
It's just another broad gate, unglinting, grey
Four horizontal bars, crossed by the diagonal
A staple binding one hedgerow to another.
But then it reaches out, starts to pull me
Towards itself, an invitation from myself
An aperture into other space which tells
Me nothing and shows me everything
Is something more, and shines there
As it hangs, this brightness
Beckoning, this teenage understanding
The gate comes back to me, unannounced
Announcing everything.

Undone

We have left undone dignity
We have left undone equality
We have left this good earth undone when we thought we
Were doing it up
We have done globalisation
And done quite well
But we have not made the connection
Between our own life and every other life.
We have done emergencies, flood and famine
Then we have gone on our way
With no time to wonder why there was an emergency.
We have done empire and are conflicted
And we have left reparations undone.
We have done white supremacy
Calling it by other names.
We have done miracles when we needed to
A vaccine in ten months not ten years
But we have left undone the miracle
When a killer virus wasn't killing us
When it was taking lives in countries far away.
We have done war while marching against it
And turned up the global thermometer while going green.
It has been subtle, under the radar
Where we shopped or who we banked with
Investments we never knew about
Because we never asked.
We have left undone the systems where the power lives.
It wasn't that we didn't think about it
Just that it was complex and the longer we umm-ed

And aaah-ed, the more we found the systems lived in us
That they had become the devices and desires in our own
Hearts.

As for the hidden holy laws that govern goodness and
Wellbeing
The deep science of mutuality and co-operation
Of balance and sustainability
The laws that find the divine image in every face
And explain mountains that break into song
Or find trees in fields of applause
And rivers that roll down in righteousness
We have offended against these laws
Although we usually didn't mean to
And often had the best of intentions.

Still, we have erred and strayed and generally got a little lost
We have left undone those things which we ought
To have done
And we have done those things which we ought not
To have done
It's not healthy for any of us

And our penitence is to do justice and love mercy
To walk more lightly on this life-giving earth
That we may hereafter live lives of courage, freedom and peace
And observe the shy glory in every living thing
Amen

A prayer for difficult people

We pray for difficult people
We are all difficult to someone, sometime
And some of us are difficult a lot of the time
To a lot of us
Some of our difficulties may fix us
And some may break us
And it is difficult to know the difference
But every day has another one
We pray for our difficulties
May they be resolved
May they resolve us
Amen

Help, thanks, wow

I put myself in her shoes.
They don't fit.
I ask myself what a life must be like
To leave it for a life like this.
In her shoes I have worn out
All my options.
Help.

For that last breath.
And this next one.
For this heart which keeps the beat,
Though I never notice.
For being here. Alive. And knowing we are.
Thanks.

For the sun and rain.
Seedtime and harvest.
On this blue-green blur of possibility
Among a hundred billion galaxies.
For the physics of gravity,
Space, time, light
Which are calculated
To be just right.
Wow!

Poem launderette

In stained, sky-blue T-shirt, the tall African-American sits on
The step
His trousers dancing elegant cartwheels behind the glass.
'Let me tell you something ...' he says, to a wire from his ear
Before being held up by a rumbling volcanic cough.
'Let me tell you something,' he starts again.
But his unseen conversationalist doesn't want to be told.
'Here's the thing ...' he tries again,
As a purple towel flies by the back of his head.

A couple, sounding Australian, in white shorts, white vests
On this warm summer's day
Unload a team of martial arts suits, from two plastic buckets,
Measure out grey detergent, pour in silver quarters,
Discuss staying, leaving, shuffle past a Latina woman,
Her green dress ebbing, flowing as she folds, refolds, a pair of
Men's jeans.
I imagine who he is, as the illuminated red counter
Tells me my countdown has counted down, my cycle spun.
I retrieve my socks, shirts, pyjamas, hesitating
Over my underpants, not wishing to embarrass them
In the bright glare of this New York afternoon.

The owner of this Chinese laundry puts down her iron,
Tells her son
To pull those sheets from the drier, the one in the top corner,
Then points to me, to it, to me, breaks my dollars into quarters
One for every six minutes and I calculate the drying-tumbling-
shrinking formula
As the man in the sky-blue T-shirt fails again

To present the thing
Coughs up the volcano, stills himself
The molten lava slowly slipping back down his throat.

Load, unload, untangle and fold
Ten of us, pirouetting this orbital day.
A newcomer unzips a supernova of a suitcase,
An unknown galaxy of alien fashion decisions breaking out
Eyes me suspiciously, decides I am looking at his smalls.
I turn away, alarmed by the thought
That my indigo linen shirt may have shrunk.
I see its sleeves, through the glass darkly,
Flailing desperately, imploring me as it
Shuffles by red polo shirt, black sock
Descending and ascending, through endless cycle.
I see how we move around each other, circling or tangled
Stretched to our limits, crumpled, unrecognised
Baptised, then dried, tired but revived.

Let me tell you something,
The Earth moves under us, anyway,
Cycling through its own orbit,
Dizzy with daily rotation,
Wondering how the sun does it
How it dances like that
How it keeps time like us, how – here's the thing –
How it spins and spins and spins.

A necessary reconciliation

At the sink, hands submerged in soapy pool,
Dishwasher redundant, on auto, scrubbing a bowl
What's this about? The question bubbles up
As if the answer is a secret from myself

Climbing the stairs, where I ask myself what
I came up here for, that pile of papers
Shuffling them like cards on the desk
That shirt, those trousers, I no longer wear

Walking them to the door where sight may
Tip off memory, next time I head to Holloway Road
Later, looking into the garden, then, gazing further
Out, into the middle distance of this life

An instant frozen, stop sign raised to passing time
Becalmed, a lull, not needing even to be needed
But aimlessness, this too will bubble up
Even nothing is usually up to something

He's been farting about all day, Marian tells me
One afternoon, soon after she and Joe are out of bed
I have not been farting about, he says, I have been pottering
And pottering is a necessary reconciliation of the mind

Seven blessings for a wedding

1.

Blessed is this earth beneath our feet (the only one we have)

2.

This being here, our daily bread
This ordinary joy, all the days ahead

3.

Blessed are we all, he, she, they,
Brothers, sisters, fathers, mothers,
Husbands, wives, partners, lovers

4.

Blessed be these vows, between this couple
To have and to hold, for richer for poorer
This making a way, this shelter of love
This human communion, all the above

5.

Blessed is the stranger, the lonely, the lost
The welcome we keep, the tea in the pot
Our down days, our up days,
Our nothing very much days
This great net of friendship in which we're all caught

6.

Blessed are our hearts, our minds, our bodies
Our jokes and laughter, our triumphs and disasters
Our waking and sleeping, veiled thoughts, deep feeling
Our drives and passion, our courage and compassion
Our rows, our fights, the bashful compromise
Finding life as a gift, learning how to be wise

7.

Blessed is this earth beneath our feet
Spinning rock of light in endless sky
Every life seeking peace, every day till we die
Blessed are those lives we no longer see
The ones who were with us and yet never leave
Blessed is the love that holds us together
To have and to hold, for ever and ever.

Two friends (wedding poem)

Two friends stand together, in the halo of the day
The halo of the impossible, the halo of the true
How everything fell out of everywhere
Then fell into place, this place
That only exists right now
With these flowers, these vows

How those who brought them here and those
Who couldn't make it, how they stand here too
How they all met, and we all meet
All those yet to walk down this earth's aisle
How this green-blue orb, idling its engines in dark space
Was only ever waiting for this one parking place

Waiting for all the things we didn't have planned
Waiting like the green blade in the buried grain
Waiting since the year dot, before the Big Bang
Since the silent music before all that began
Since the invention of love, a universal communion
For this song and reading and mystic union

Two friends stand together in the halo of the day
This halo now
With the altar and the rings
This love now
That binds every everything

Name-drop

Damien Hirst, you know, spot paintings
Formaldehyde, dead sharks,
Once I shared a lift with him.
He pretended not to recognise me.

I sat at a table with Banksy
But no-one told me it was him till later
This must be how he manages to be
Celebrated everywhere
For being completely unknown.

I shook hands with Bill Gates
When he was the world's richest person
I had prepared an anecdote, in advance,
In which I asked to borrow a fiver
But I missed my cue.

I passed Martin Sheen on Oxford Street
But it may not count, it was before
He'd moved into the West Wing as President Josiah Bartlet
By the time I'd realised he was not an old friend,
Whose name I couldn't place,
He was already not being recognised,
By other people, down by John Lewis.

One day I was standing by a zebra crossing,
Off Marylebone Road,
When overcome with certainty
That I was acquainted with the older man next to me,
Waiting for a pause in the traffic,
I turned and said, *'Are you who I think you are?'*

Which, granted, was a difficult question
As I wasn't thinking he was, say, Derren Brown,
So how could he know who I was thinking I thought he was?
'Who do you think I am?'
I said, Van Morrison, the singer
Although I didn't say 'the singer' to him
Only to you, in case you don't know
How famous he is, to me.
'Yes,' he said, before walking away,
As if we weren't intimate companions
Hadn't been so often into the mystic
And shared the beautiful vision.
For a second, I admit,
I thought our paths had crossed for a purpose
That we might become friends,
That he would appreciate my work
As I did his
But he was never back in touch.

Waiting at a bus stop on the way home from work
A car paused for the lights and I saw these eyebrows
Elevating on a face in the back seat,
Looking out into the drizzle.
It was Salman Rushdie, the novelist, who was supposed to be
In hiding.
I walked out towards him, waving a friendly wave
(I might have had a drink)
But my friendly gesture was lost in translation
As a plain-clothes security officer leapt out
Of the front seat, charging at me, to protect the novelist
In case I'd been trying to deliver
A fatwa on Clerkenwell Road.

I recall the car speeding him off back into hiding,
As I took the No. 63 in plain sight back to King's Cross.

Ava introduced me to Oprah
And Desmond Tutu introduced me to Jesus Christ
(Even though I thought we'd already met)
Kate Winslet lived in a flat at the end of our street
Before *Titanic* took her to the country.
Walking back from Holloway Road, I used to whisper to Meg
'Don't look now, it's her …'
But Meg never saw her like me
Sometimes I think we look at
People completely differently.

Why do I look twice at them
As if what they have, we need
To make us complete
While looking straight through and beyond
All these other people
Whose stories go unrecognised
The man flipping burgers in the fast-food joint
A lawyer in his home country
Before fleeing for his life
The woman chattering to herself in the street
Who delivered your babies
Long ago, when she was a midwife
The elderly man, in front of you in the queue,
Taking ages to count out change for his *Daily Mail*
He used to fight fires, saving innocent lives
Even now it can keep him awake all night.

The friendship

We do not know, cannot predict
In this crowd of all the living
How some of us connect and click
To be friends is all thanksgiving

We may not always share a view
We stand in such a different place
What is it that draws me to you
True friendship is a state of grace

When I don't buy your argument
You fail to read my eloquence
I do not doubt your true intent
Your spirit has a resonance

We harbour loss and anchor pain
Sink the ship, refloat, get on
Feel the breeze, set sail again
Caught up in this phenomenon

We're only here a little while
It takes a life to take life in
The daily quiz, the question why
Love and friendship are everything

Dear friend, this is some alchemy
Each new day a sacred space
We choose to live them gratefully
True friendship is a state of grace

The name

The name beyond all names
The name we are all called and do not know
The name before names were invented
The name of all the life we cannot take in

The name is earth crumbling like dust in your hands,
Talking to you, instructing you
This is you also, from dust, to dust
The name is a mother holding her child
This wordless faith, this limitless love
The name is a friend, talking someone down from suicide bridge
The name is turning down the money
The name is not religious, may not believe
The name is a cleaner in a hospital corridor
The one we never noticed, wiping up the puke
The name has hoovered the office, two hours before we arrived
The name is in prison, over the road
Visiting someone who shall be nameless,
And never gets a visit

The name is nameless too sometimes
The name is long out of touch with who she was
Calling for her cat in the street
'Here, puss, here, puss ...'

Calling out to love and company and another sense of all things
The name is stopping to remember that someone you loved
Is no longer alive
The name of God is not God
God isn't enough for all of this
And all of that
The name beyond all names
Hallowed be thy name

Bow

Perhaps a bow is the way to go
Now shaking hands is in the past
And brushing elbows, a little daft

Perhaps we'll meet in common space
Take in each other, break into a smile
Catch our breath, it's been a while

Perhaps we'll sense the depth of all this
Holding the wonder of here and now
If we pause. And stop. And bow

The four Presidents

On the day of the Inauguration
Just like The President said
History zigzagged
A wave rippled in the Atlantic,
On its east, when everyone was looking west
When people were packing to leave, fearing war
The President's fingers were loosened
His grip on power released
Just as The President had asked us to believe
Not in his ability to bring about change
But in ours, The President finally bowed
To the will of the people and stood down
'I submit myself only to the judgement of Allah,' he said
'Whose judgement is beyond time and history'
As he boarded a plane, holding a one-way ticket to exile
And most of his country's cash
The President put his hand on two Bibles,
Thanking the other Presidents in attendance,
From now on, he said, this country will be First,
This great country will be protected by God
The President, watching history zig, looked at The President,
Knowing that history will also zag, and The President said
'We will build a country where what you know
Counts for more than who you know and there will be
No discrimination on the basis of gender, religion or ethnic
Origin'
And The President allowed himself a brief memory
Of his days as a security guard at Argos, on The Holloway Road
And so it was that on the day of the Inauguration
Just like The President said,
History zigzagged.

Love remix

Love is steady, always ready
Love is kindness, a certain lightness
Love is unflappable, patience palpable
Love is faithful, all kinds of graceful
But
Love is truthful, not seeking approval
Love is courageous, disadvantageous
Love is awkward, not quite straightforward
Love is forgiveness, a difficult business
And
Love is dangerous, hazardous, perilous
Love is exhausting, not so rewarding
Love is impossible, irrational, implausible
Love is immeasurable, unquantifiable
But
Love is the neighbour, and also the stranger
Love is extraordinary, disguised as the ordinary
Love is the doing, whatever the feeling
Love the direction, despite the distraction
And
Love is the whole and also the broken
Love is being held and also the holding
Love is subversion, goodness and mercy
Love is the mystery, empowering history

But
Love is shy, not me, myself, I
Love is mischievous, a wink of the eye
Love is discreet, not swagger or bragger
Love the connection from paying attention
And
Love is the debit, not looking for credit
Love the economy of some other society
Love is the debt we owe to each other
Love the exchange rate that never depreciates
But
Love is straight-talking, a difficult word
Love is tuned in to those not being heard
Love is the kindness but also the justice
Love is the word when love is the verb
And
Love is the risk, it may not come off
Love is the heart and the falling apart
Love is the grief, the loss, no relief
Love is the wound, inside me, inside you
But
Love is looking out, for those we can't see
Love is the shelter, I give you, you give me
Love is the promise not broken by death
Love is the hope that all will be well

Steadying myself

Every day is moving
Destabilising
Each new one stamped
With a health and safety warning
Talking with someone
Then, walking on down the street
I stop myself
Lean against a wall
Sit down.

Some days I have to stop this moving life
To receive it
As if everything is trying to explain itself to me
All at once and in these
Faint and distant scintillas
Lost inside fragments of seconds
I know how briefly and beautifully
We are here
How deep still calls to deep
Even if deep doesn't know how to reply
And I steady myself to continue

But sometimes
I fall down.

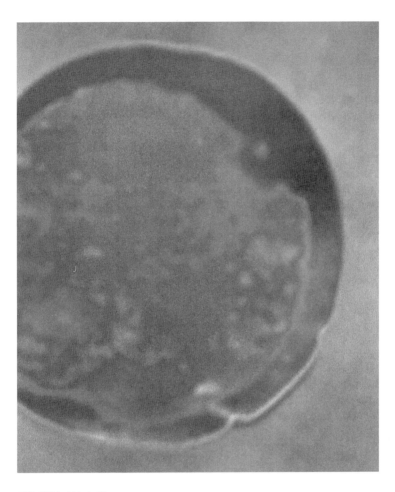

EVENING

Sweet right foot

I was not able to give you the gift of mathematics
The gift of music
The gift of patience and kindness
They came from somewhere else in the gene pool
Maybe it was nurture not nature
But I like to believe that one of my genes
Has slipped from my generation to yours
A sweet right foot
With a shot
Like no other
A bullet into the top right-hand corner
An unstoppable volley from halfway up the pitch
A rasping screamer from an impossible distance
Leaving opponent and teammate
Quietly respectful
A sweet right foot
Treasure it, enjoy it
It will comfort you on many occasions
Give thanks
That came from me

Talking church

All quiet, I unlocked your doors, discreetly broke in.
Not to disturb you, interfere with that frequency
I so rarely tune to. I sat down by the font,
Held a second in my palm, dialled the silence,
Awaited communication, some kind of guidance,
The font was tight-lipped.

The rood screen blanked me, I tried not to take it personally.
The organ, holding her breath, was not coming up for air.
I looked for my words to speak to the unspoken,
Locked down in quiet time, this great crowd of witness.
What are you thinking? I whispered, on the chancel,
Where the candles played dead, keeping their distance.

Mary winked from the window, with a stained-glass eye
Splintering the sun from ninety-three million miles.
Do you miss us? I asked. Do you want us back? An angel
Arched an eyebrow, advised I stop talking,
Said silence holds more than quiet, that the absence of
All souls doesn't mean they're not here.

I lay down in the nave, gazed up through the dust motes,
At the pillars, the arches, the old wooden roof,
Heard a chorus of voices, singing someone's death
Witnessed a happy couple, plighting their troth
Saw heads being bowed, knees being bent, forgiveness
And mercy and centuries of weeping. And someone,
From the future, came to offer me the peace.

She said, this house is open, even when it's closed
Prayers pray themselves, that's how everything goes.

Hold it in the light

Hands together, eyes closed
Sit quite still, breathe real slow
Take this moment to find your life
Hold it in the light

Hold a friend, hold them here
All the ones you hold so dear
Hold them in your heart and mind
Hold them in the light

Hold that hurt, a wound you know
Hold it there, then let it go
Whatever it is, whatever it was
Hold them in the light

Hold your street, your town, your world
The good news and the bad
The forgotten and the overlooked
Hold them in the light

Hold your hope, and your despair
Capture them inside a prayer
Take this moment, find your life
Hold it in the light

Boomerang

For every welcome,
Hello,
The unsettling goodbye
You pick someone up,
From bus or train
Doorbell rings,
Here they are.
Again.

For all the anticipation,
Still,
You can't bury
The thought,
Soon you'll be dropping them off.
Again.

The orbit of the boomerang expands
In time, flies out of sight
It may not always return
You have only yourself to blame
The life you gave them
Is no longer yours
And still
It is, and always will be.

Our joy is encircled by grief
Our grief encircled by joy.
Everything encircled by something else
That none of us can name.

Behind her back
Happiness
Holds hands with
Sadness

We do not avoid these bittersweet days
By never leaving
Only
By never arriving.

Glad tidings

I'd fallen for it, been taken in
Everyone saying how you don't exist
That you're not with us any more
That, probably, you never were
More than a literary device
To bring glad tidings from one dimension
To another, a promise of extra resources
When times are tough, a workout
For Jacob, company for
Shadrach, Meshach and the other one

But last Wednesday it dawned on me
The way you dawned on hillside shepherds
Out of nothing and in tune with
Everything. That's it
Is what I thought, that's what
I would do, if I were you

If I was an angel in this world today
I would lie myself like a prayer
On the roof of every house
Inhaling light like life
Because light and life to all she brings

I would dance on the green hillsides
Raising my arms in praise of everything
Conducting the breeze like I could hear
The chords of life, that distant symphony
A gentle, unheard history

I would tiptoe along the bowl edge
Of the blue horizon, teasing the tides
Pedalling the waves, like this energy was
Renewable as love, and the more we shared it
The more we generated

Now I see you silent
On pavement pole-top
Praying for conversion
Of daylight into nightlight
And solitary mystic, humming
Slow hymns by the motorway
And massed choral voices singing the climb
Of the mountains, lifting us, surely,
From these shadowed valleys

I see you
Commanding the wind and the waves
Not to be still, this time
But to blow us all
To kingdom come

Humming

Sometimes singing
Sometimes humming
Alone with yourself, complete
In your own company
Which means content which is
A version of happy which is
A relative of joy which is
(like love or courage, tears or laughter)
Among the ways I divine the divine
The one Eckhart said is like
Someone who coughs, while hiding
Or sings to herself, or hums
While pruning a bush
Or filling the dishwasher

Talking in the garden
I look up, from my book, and notice,
There is no person for you to be talking to
And that you are not talking to yourself
But to the chickens
Which is surreal only on the surface
Further down, under the grass, under the earth
Under the below of everything
Way deep down it is peace and friendship
With this living world and its creatures
And further down still it is a memory
Of how things will be
One day, of how things were once
Long ago, in another garden
Sometimes singing
Sometimes humming

The parable of the woman on my old bike

I am in the alley at the side of the house
The spare space where we put the things we can't quite
agree we won't need again
The space we visit in the spare days, like today, the ones
between Christmas and New Year

Into a plastic bag of cables and plugs, I am adding a
superfast broadband router which has now been outrun
These cables charge phones that we no longer have
Or time-saving garden devices which will trim the nostril hair
at the edge of a lawn
Devices which slowed everything down because their batteries
were always flat

Leaning into the antique coal bin left by the previous owners
a quarter century ago, in their fossil-fuelled world
I am picking out lumps of coal from dark dunes of dust
We can warm ourselves from these on one of the
eleven days we lay a fire in our front room
The central heating never looks as good

A cobwebbed axe head is missing a handle
The vicious teeth of a circular blade are brown and
rusting
These plastic boxes of press cuttings peer at me anxiously
We both know that whenever I stop over them they are one
sling closer to the recycling bin
But also that it's always, not quite time

This bicycle has moved me from A to B across the A
to Z
I compose a sign to hang on its handlebars
'Please take away. Needs slow puncture repaired and WD-40'

In the alley at the side of our house I recite my creed
I believe in the Islington Household Reuse and Recycling
Centre
I believe that my glass bottles will be separated and sent to
facilities for processing into glass cullet or pellets, to make more
bottles, or road surfaces
I believe this sticky tin that once held tomatoes may one day
encase a laptop or become the stem of a traffic light
That these Christmas cards and free newspapers will be born
again as Christmas cards and free newspapers
I believe that this radio, like other small electrical appliances,
will be dismantled, separated into metal and plastic and find a
new life holding together a mobile phone or decorating
someone's ears
I believe that yoghurt pots and fruit punnets, foil-lined cartons
and shower gel bottles will live again next to margarine tubs
and cooking oil containers, with only a ghostly memory of the
life they once lived
I believe that this woman freewheeling down our road is a
parable
That the spinning orbs that carry her are the engines that
power mystery
I believe she saw the sign and is on my old bike
I believe that upcycling is a form of resurrection

Only disconnect

We give thanks for the failure of the wireless connection
The network that is down
The password we've forgotten

For the reminder of how to search our own minds,
The miracle of local attention
A facial expression
Someone's question

We give thanks for the gift of being unavailable
Except to the person who is adjacent
For the mealtime when the device is uninvited,
The fast when we learned how to wait
And discovered that to wait is to see

We confess to the attraction of distraction
The illusion that information is power
That knowledge is wisdom
That facts will save us

We give thanks for the invisible networks
On the days when we only disconnect

The evolution of the rota

We give thanks for the evolution of the rota
Clandestine strip along which kindness motors
Genius sequence no scientist has unravelled
Mutuality, the genome less travelled

How the meeting is chaired and the chairs put out
The coffee served and the mugs washed up
The teams are picked, everyone gets a lift
Someone on their own gets a surprise visit

A life is changed, an hour on the helpline
Nervous young reader gets a little more time
The beds are weeded, the grass cut
Volunteering at the breakfast club
The demo takes place, the placard, the paint
Grown-ups make their point, kids entertained
Food arrives at the Shelter, tables laid
Everyone full and nobody pays

Noticeboard, spreadsheet, annoying text
Your name comes up – *'Don't forget'*
Duty and kindness, mind and heart
In the grand scheme of everything
This is our small part

In this hidden economy, time is not money
And no-one ever uses the word reciprocity
Her turn, his turn, their turn, my turn,
The rota turns, a new world discerned
It goes around, this modest institution
This cycle of goodness, this gentle revolution.

What religion smells like

Early on a cold Sunday morning in the first quarter of the year
I walk up the road and turn left
Into the garden of the church
Pace ten grey slabs of the weathered path and enter
By a narrow opening,
One great oak door heaved back from the other.

Leaving behind the day's first rays
The dim-lit lobby messages another sense
Sight now competing with smell
Bacon, eggs, eau de cologne
The common tang of one holy faith
The real presence in toast and ketchup
In plates wiped clean, of yolk and baked beans.

Walking through the incense of this fine faith
I turn left down the nave to find a seat
At the chancel, between someone with a home
And someone who's lost one
She who minutes ago left the soft bosom of family
He who slept on this hard floor all night
I raise my head, inhale resignation and courage
The meeting of our days
Life reacting with life
This invisible chemistry

I will not smell the gifts of bread and wine
When they arrive
But we will know them in another sense
As we know the sacred scent in all good gifts
The pungent holy ghost of a winter night shelter
The fleeting aroma of another kind of world
The smell of true religion.

Through line

Light rises, we slowly come to
What is this? What happens next?
Where am I and, come to that, who?
Gradually, life starts to make sense

We rise, our lines now coming back
Bleary-eyed, we fall into the light
Everyone else is already here
Swept up in the movement of life

Every new scene is a riddle
Gift-wrapped and bow-tied in mystery
Every new act an enigma
This serial drama called history

Does anyone know the narrative arc?
Or even what's coming up next?
This long-running show that we're in
That every day gets recommissioned

Light falls, we retreat to ourselves
Another day, still not found out
Lying in the dark, what was that all about,
Looking for the through line of love

Middle tint

I had never heard of 'middle tint'
Until you quoted John Ruskin, observing
How the most skilful of painters
Devote most of their canvas to this

It sounds like an English village, Middle Tint,
Or a prescription for new glasses; in fact,
You write, it's everything we take for granted
Each ordinary day, this overlooked life

There is excessively small quantity, said Ruskin
Of extreme light and extreme shade, all the
Mass of the picture being graduated, delicate
Middle tint, laid before dark colours, before light

The going back and fore, to school, to work
The paying of bills, small joys, hidden hurts
The spag bol on Monday, the washing, the ironing
The colleague who dislikes you, a cloud, no silver lining
A tooth that needs filling, distant conflict, all that killing
Those thoughts in the night, morning sunlight
Words spoken in haste, a friendship that breaks
The clink of the glasses, the moment that passes
Ambition that's thwarted, most things that get sorted
Dirty mugs in the sink, all this, the middle tint

This is what you wrote, Lauren F Winner
How middle tint is our rote, unshowy behaviour
We may not see it, but it's most of the canvas

Our eyes drawn instead to
Birth, marriage and death
Maybe this is prayer, most of the time, and going
To church, the length of a life, and against this
Great landscape – the joy and the gloom –
A bush flares into flame,
And someone,
Illuminated,
Walks away from a tomb

The Age of Poignant

The phone call comes, confirming our foreboding
Is there hope in the email, can we decode it?
Beneath our feet the ground is unreliable
Welcome to the Age of I'd-like-to-deny-it-all

We are living in the Age of Poignant
Now weeping is our primary employment
Now no-one need touch us for us to feel touched
And our hands hold the day like dust

We are living in the Age of Bittersweet
Love and loss arm in arm on the street
Now all our clever words have disappeared
And we're left with the language of tears

We are living in the Golden Hour
Light burnishing every face
We wear our hearts on our sleeve every day
They are waiting to be broken again

What I think I am doing when I am praying

It occurred to me that you might not know
what I think I am doing
When I am sitting here like this, or lying on the bed like that
Or, come to think of it,
when I am running or waiting for a bus

I'm not sure if it can be explained but perhaps I can describe it
What we are doing, when we say the name of a child
who has lost a parent,
or the name of a friend who is in trouble
When we mention that country where the rain will not arrive
Or that one which everyone is running from,
how we name them
arriving in small boats, to be arrested in this one

Or why we sit here without saying anything,
when we could be being productive,
making things or planning
Why I am looking at that candle,
wondering if there is a
language of flame

Over-thinking again, when all we are really doing is stopping
the day,
to hold it for a moment, a little more carefully,
although,
we might say sorry,
for dropping it again, yesterday

There are words we may turn to, well-practised, tried, tested
For all those times when our own can't meet the moment
Those times when you hold the day
and it falls to pieces in your hands

It might begin with an asking, but, later, below the detail
what you notice is really a longing, a wordlessness
Or just a faint beat
The pulse of a world described by silence or grief,
by music or joy

To be honest, I must tell you, it works, it really does
In the way of a walk along the shore, or a song,
when the words return
In the way of goodness which will not be weighed
or measured
Or how
someone can be with you after their death
It works in a way you hadn't guessed
And of course, it doesn't work either,
not in the ways of cause and effect
that I can explain to you,
but it definitely works
Not least as way of explaining my life to my life
A bit like this, in a way

Hubbub

This cold night, this darkness
And clinking of glasses
The what are you having?
And talk about nothing
The stories, the laughter
This life as it passes
These friends and this pint
Unlocking this life
The warmth of the pub
This wonder-fuelled hubbub

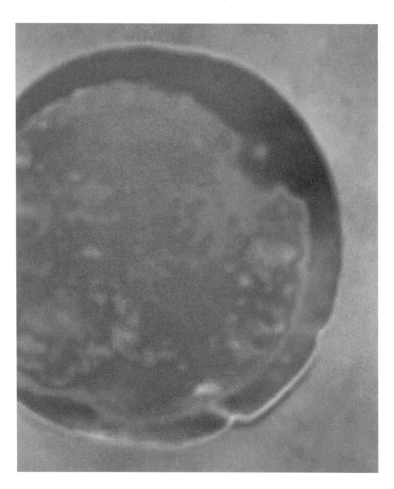

NIGHT

My feet

My feet are wrapped around yours
Your feet are wrapped around mine
Where do you end and where do I begin
Now that we can no longer see
How we have grown into each other?

When the weather turns
And I am not blown over
And I remain standing
I recall this understorey
Where we have planted our life
How our roots are grown together
Under the duvet

Cairn

This bookshelf is a cairn piled high
The quiet retreat where I stand alone

With all these others who came this way
Mulling on the mystery of one more day

At all the trouble we go to explain it
And the silence that greets our failure

I stand in the ruination of words
And praise their endless daring

I lay another prayer on the pile
Adding to history's intercession

Swallow

Cycling the wind
Up the hill of the world
Until the first swift catches up
With the first swallow

Your climb is long too
Tired, unsleep, on the wing
But soon, swift
Soon, swallow

Harbour

My nautical friend speaks a lexicon
Of port and starboard, wave and wind.
He is tacking right now, leaning into the weather
He saw coming before the rest of us.
This sky lowering itself to bruise the earth.
And once it's all mist and spray and we lose
Each other, he has another sight, to navigate
Safe passage, until we see those sails again,
Until we all find harbour.

Flight mode

I have put my life on flight mode
And I see how others travel
How they ride hidden currents
Dive through weather patterns
Packing lightly to cross a world
And its seasons, singing
Now
As they arrive
In the air above me
Tails ruddering the breeze
Quizzing me from the silent encyclopaedia
Of this wide sky
Tweeting
As if they'd thought of it first

Rehearsal

Mind if I try this one more time?
Retake that scene, rewrite those lines

That dialogue, it isn't me
It isn't who I want to be

I'd never have taken on that part
I'd never mean to break your heart

And that thing I always meant to say?
I'm ready now. I'll speak today

Life's not an act, it isn't staged
It's improv and an empty page

This dance in time, this wild delight
This practice that will take a life

We get it wrong, that's universal
Each new day the next rehearsal

Take one, take two, take three, take four
Now let me try it, just once more

Shiver

'Wind of the spirit'
Says the good book
More often a draught
Shiver on the neck
Or ankle.
Source unknown
Keeping me awake

Wasted

When do we decide
We are old enough
That how old we feel
Is how old we are

(The body, breaking down
Raises a comic eyebrow
Over the mind's
Furious denial)

We will never be as old as our parents
Who were never as young as us
To our children we may not reveal
How little we know
How young we feel

That we would welcome youth
Being wasted on us again
Or evidence of the wisdom
The years are said to return us

That we would like to be
Old enough to know better
And young enough to still believe

The text which cannot be answered

No sooner has it arrived than I feel the text
    looking me in the eye
Urging me to find the right reply, the one we both know
    isn't possible
If the right reply is ever to exist, it will not fit on this screen
It may not even fit in this life, but still, the text looks at me
The text which cannot be answered, and must be

Don't blame yourself, little phone, it's not your fault
You've been made to believe you can do anything,
To process life immediately when (I must text you)
Some news cannot be processed in less than five years,
    often longer
You've been designed for the instant reply
But for some messages there are no instant replies,
For some messages there are no replies

You mean well, and thank you, for recognising the places
    where words end
Thumbs up for the emotional abbreviation of emoji and
    emoticon
But they end too, they cannot capture who I am
The body language and verbal tone
The distant planets inside myself, desperate to make contact
    with earth
The speechlessness pouring from this mouth,
    these rubbed-red-raw eyes

When my friend's message arrives and says,
Sorry to bring you this news …
    they say there's nothing to be done
I want some simple semiotic that replies
I haven't got an expression for this
Some digital sign which is the pause before I speak
Which becomes the silence when I don't
Which is the writer looking at the blank page
Understanding that to say nothing is all there is to say

On other days I want an emoticon which genuflects
In your dazzling radiance next to me
Which stands within the golden halo of a tree
    and is saturated with your real presence
I want an emoji that has run out of ways of trying to say
    what this is
Every day, every night,
Which walks its own talk, which walks me over the bridge
    between my virtue signalling and my virtue
Which is wise as a poem but not too clever by half

I want an emoji for the days which carry no word
    of their own explanation,
Where I have never met the feeling I'm supposed to feel
Some way of sending joy to the world,
Without it being misunderstood as happiness

I want an emoticon which is the face of Ahmed
Sitting in Costa, adjusting his position all the time

Because of the injuries he carries from the war he fled,
Talking to his parents on FaceTime
In a village beside a Syrian sea,
The village he may not see again,
The parents he may not hold again.

I don't want an emoji worth a thousand words
Only a small sign for my outside
That gives you a clue about what's going on in my inside.

A blessing for a time when the words are gone

That you will share the richest conversation
Even when the sentence trails off, the thought is lost

That you will speak the truths that words can carry
And let your looking toward each other say all the rest

That a dark humour will mark your furious defiance
Your laughter remind you how joy will find a way

That as you go through this – now there is no way around –
You will know deep company, when you are most alone

That you will hear each other across the sound of
sadness
Make each other out through the mist of tears

That your friendship will be fluent as the trees through
the window
As the dog's warm breath, cupped in your hand

That this broken-hearted ordinary may now and then
transfigure itself
And you find yourselves for ever in a numinous now

Love started talking in the conversation you first begun
It cannot be ended, even when all the words are gone

Hashtag Amen

In 1949, they were caught, in a haystack,
In each other's arms.
He was still in her arms
When he died,
64 years later. #Amen

Lovely kid. Clever. Musical.
Drinking by 13. Couldn't stop. 30 yrs.
Dead. In his flat.
We loved him. We lost him. #Amen

We don't want anything religiousy.
He wasn't religious at all.
Can we have The Lord's Prayer? #Amen

Wally, 90, blows his last trumpet.
Sent him out with April in Paris, Count Basie Big Band
& Dedication to Joy, Tubby Hayes Quartet. #Amen

He'd be asking everyone,
'Where's the party afterwards?'
If this wasn't his own
Funeral. #Amen

Reg used to parachute
From high
In the deep blue sky
Over enemy lines.
Today, his last jump,
he landed behind
friendly lines. #Amen

She weeps in grief.
Can't read her poem
To Gran.
He steps up. Holds her steady.
Calm, she reads.
Love will not be buried. #Amen

1945. A dance. Their eyes met.
Married 65 years.
She died @82. Broken-hearted,
4 days later, @88, he died too.
Buried 2gether 2day. #Amen

The delivery

The silhouette, through the glass, is visible
But the delivery will not fit
The package cannot be delivered
No letterbox was made for this

You turn, at the sound, as the door crashes down
The reaction that's only delayed
The breaking news that's breaking you
The delivery that takes away

We cannot receive the impossible
The news that cannot be true
We cannot receive what we cannot believe
That a heart can be broken in two

We cannot call, we cannot write
These tears are our best reply
Some clichés are real but time will not heal
We cannot undo this goodbye

We write without words in the half-light
Our thoughts draw the lines of a prayer
Here you are, once again, like you're with us
Invisible, improbable as air.

Dark

You are the dark of the world
When all is brightness and dazzle

You are a deepening mystery
When life is a surfeit of solutions

You are the nagging doubt and secret sceptic
When everyone believes so much

You are jangling discord, right out of tune
When all the sounds are harmony

You are the abstract art of paint and poem
When our propaganda makes everything clear

You are the parched throat, the desert defeat
When there's water, water everywhere

You are the silent absence, gone-missing god
When the cacophony of belief becomes deafening

You are uncharted journey, road less travelled
When we're all mapped out. Been there, done that

You are the stranger in the night, throwing us to the ground
When all we want to do is get away

You are the cloud of unknowing
When we know-it-alls know it all

You are never ready and take for ever
When we want it now and cannot wait

You are the dark of the world
When all is brightness and dazzle

Wave

We hold invisible hands with those
who have gone down in history
and are risen in glory
We stand beside those
who have disappeared from view
and now see more than ever
We embrace those we never met
who will be our friends for ever
We are the mere mortals
who mass, restless, on eternal hillsides
oblivious to our true identity, our great companions.

Look once, or twice, then look again
See Patrick and Brigid talking with Jesus
Óscar Romero with Dorothy Stang
while Manche Masemola, Rumi and Anne Frank
are laughing ... with Martin Luther King

There's William Blake talking to Rachel Corrie
And Mahalia Jackson with Hildegard of Bingen
And didn't that woman used to serve you in Tesco?
She's with the prophet Amos, he's listening

John O'Donohue and Eckhart are speaking in tongues
with Olaudah Equiano and Gustavo Parajón

and Julian of Norwich, who's got the kettle on
And these are some whose lives we know
Others we don't, they are yet to be born.
Yet all are among us, beside us, everywhere around us
This wave rolling
backwards and forwards through time,
this great cloud of witness
clocking in, clocking out, in daily duty
to that fleeting commonwealth
But our moment is here, for all moments are now
We hold invisible hands with those
who have gone down in history
We cannot let go
They are holding us

War

Bring us peace though we act like war
Bring us kindness though we try to hoard the world
Bring us friendship though we misjudge the stranger
Bring us freedom though we tie ourselves in knots
Bring us stillness though we want to keep moving
Bring us faith though we have all these doubts
Bring us wisdom though we pretend to know it all
Bring us peace though we act like war

Dust

Even though we must
Remember we are dust
And to dust we shall return
We have these bright days
As we walk on this clay
To make ourselves, make ourselves up

Even though each day
Will often go wrong
And sometimes never goes right
Nothing's done and dusted
As we burn up this life
Morning to midday to night

Some days we know
There's more to all this
From darkness and stardust we're drawn
The earth finds a voice
Some words in the dust
Hold on to each other, hold on

Even though we grieve
At losing each other
Ask ourselves what it's all for
We dust ourselves down
And dust ourselves off
Compose this life once more, once more

Even though we don't
Stay as long as we want
When all's done and dusted, there's love
From ashes to ashes
And dust to dust
Love makes us all, makes us all up

Even though we must
Remember we are dust
And our end is always in sight
Forgiveness and kindness
Faith, hope and love
Will always compose a good life

Wonder

This afternoon I left you all
Seems like yesterday I first got here

Recently we had a baby girl
Today she graduated from uni

A few hours after crying goodbye to Mum at the school gate
I cried goodbye to Mum in the church pew

A moment ago I was holding him carefully lest I drop him
Now I disappear inside his hug

Every morning I struggle to tie up these shoelaces
Every morning I struggle to tie up these shoelaces

We were out on our first date the other night
Early days but we're still together

This afternoon the eldest read his marriage vows
Last night we were reading to him on his bed

The walk with you toward your grave is the same walk
As the walk down the aisle when I was your best man

Perhaps this is all happening at once, perhaps time is circular
What goes around comes around. What is it to be alive?

This afternoon I left you all
Seems like yesterday I first got here

Dear Life

Dear Life and all your joysandsadnesses
Kindness, hopefulness, lightness, darkness,
The loss or the laughter, the impossible surprise
How we make it all up, how we improvise

Dear Life and all your crumbly earthiness
These bodies that bruise, these cells that die
These veins, this blood, this beat, this heart
How we pad across the earth, and dream we might fly

Dear Life and all the stars in your sky
How we look up at night, how we wonder why
The immeasurable distance, the impossible view
How the light comes so far before reaching our eye

Dear Life and all your ordinariness
This laboratory of hours, this experiment with breath
This test tube testament of trial and error
How we try to love each other, try to be our best

Dear Life and all the people we become
The families that make us, hold us or break us
The light on the path when we're all alone
The journeys that change us, every place called home
This good luck and bad luck, this guaranteed uncertainty
This road less travelled, this place we never meant to be
Every place we found shelter, every good soul on the way

Dear Life in all your can't-take-it-inness
This impossible existence, this question mark of beingness
The languages we can't speak, like dog and tree

Like woman and man, like land and sea
Like stranger and friend, like you and me
The shoulders we stand on, the enigma of ancestry
The judgements of history, the DNA lottery
This agony, this beauty, this urgent intensity
The practice of love and the chaos theory
The baffle of questions, that will never be solved
The quest for meaning, all that's unresolved

Dear Life and all our ruin and calamity
How we hold all this pain, that no-one understands
The tangle in our mind, the ache in our heart
How we hold each other tight, then find we're torn apart
The bitterness of memories that won't let us go
The ways we are wounded, how we walk so slow
How we pull ourselves together, try not to give up
How some days hold a miracle and others hit us like a truck

Dear Life and all this good company
This here, this now, this human electricity
This theory of everything, and how to practise nothing
All this living and moving, in which we have our being
This longing to be held, this longing to hold
How we try to tell this story that can never be told

Dear Life and all your sweet-and-bitter-sweetness
The accident and illness, the unforeseen circumstance
The sliding doors, the lives that we missed
All the misunderstandings, the things we never meant
The folk we never knew, the ones who came and went
These five rich senses that speak of all the rest
This well of compassion, this spring that's never spent

Dear Life and all the ways that we age
These mottled hands, these stories on our palms
The creaks and leaks, and lines on our face
The clothes we once wore, the days of our hair

Dear Life and our fear of the end of the line
The days we never guessed at, this gratitude and grief
The mercy of kindness, the absolution of time
How we're rescued by love, whatever our belief

Dear Life and all your dazzlingmystery
Dear Life, Dear All, Dear Me, Dear You
A prayer, a sign, some shy synchronicity
Some days all we ask for is some kind of clue

Start

Whatever it was or is
Whatever it will be
The exceptional or commonplace
The misjudgement, the mistake
The completely out of character
The remorse, the embarrassment
The blown fuse, the unlike you
The bolt from the blue
The everything we never meant
The unintended consequence
The cock-up or conspiracy
The slip of the tongue
The hard-to-believe
The regret, the pain
The sorrow, the shame
Whatever it was or is
Whatever it will be
All of us can start again

A travelling blessing

May the road rise up to meet you
And the potholes never bring you down to meet the road
May the wind be at your back
Only when you've remembered to put on your thermals
May the sun shine warm upon your face
Neither burning your nose, nor the tips of your ears
And the rain fall soft on your fields
On the day when you are wearing sensible footwear
May God hold you in the palm of her hand
Never breaking into applause nor mistaking you for a stress ball

May the shortcut never be taken
Because the picturesque route would make you late
And the satnav never deprive you
Of all you might have learned off the beaten track
May you find protection in every collision,
Company in every jam
Among those who have broken down
And those who are breaking up
May you lose all sense of direction
When you end up travelling the wrong way
And find yourself completely lost only in the place
Where someone you didn't know you were looking for
Is already waiting to find you

May whatever goes wrong
Go wrong in all the right ways
And whatever goes right
Stay with you in case you end up here again
May your blind alleys bring you sight
And your dead ends new life
And a speed camera never capture you
On the path of least resistance
May your compass always point home
And your heart be inviting you to set off again
Not long after you've arrived.

Unfold

Inside the silence
Under the sound
All who are lost
All who are found
Open the day of all that
She holds
As every sweet moment
Unfolds

Hallowed

Our Mother which art in heaven
Our parents who walked this earth
Our sisters and brothers
Our partners and lovers
Hallowed be all of thy names
Amen

BACK STORIES

A mystic and visionary and the author of the first book by a woman in the English language, Julian of Norwich is also the earliest known Norwich supporter. In one of her periodic transcendent moments, holding a hazelnut in the palm of her hand, she realised, in the way that mystics do, that this little hazelnut was … everything. I had a parallel transcendent moment bending low below the sink to lift the lid of the compost bin.

Here are some other back stories.

For a quarter century I've played football every Thursday with a group of men who remain considerably younger in their minds than in their bodies. Over time some of us have had our own kids and 'Sweet right foot' was written for Wes, our eldest, when I realised I might have actually passed on to him something that would bring him real joy.

I knew nothing about the American academic Lauren F Winner when I was drawn by its title into her book *Still: Notes on a Mid-Faith Crisis* (Bravo Ltd). Being married to a painter but never understanding how painters see things, one thought stayed with me, when Lauren F Winner described how 19th-century art critic John Ruskin had suggested that most of the canvas in the great landscape paintings is *'middle tint'* – average, overlookable – but becomes spectacular by how it contains the more striking extremes of dark and light. In doing that, a great painting imitated nature herself. Likewise for the believer, said Lauren F Winner, calling 'middle tint' the *'palette of faithfulness'*. Most of the time humdrum, ordinary, workaday but on the odd day … everything is lit up.

The poem 'Dark' took on an unexpected afterlife when the singer-songwriter Luke Sital-Singh called to say he'd turned it into a song and hoped I didn't mind. I didn't. Later I tuned in to an episode of the reality TV series *Made in Chelsea* to hear the song on the soundtrack. Later still on the American TV drama *Suits*. The song is still buying me new poetry books.

Another poem in this collection, 'Here comes the day', found an afterlife as a song by Martyn Joseph on his recent album *1960* (Pipe Records), along with a couple of other lyrics which are not in this collection.

Lines from 'Wave', which I read at the Galway memorial for John O'Donohue in 2008, found another kind of new life. Someone on that day asked for permission to take the last lines and have them carved in rock at a memorial site somewhere else in Ireland. (I forget where, but I've seen the photos.)

'I lift up my eyes (lockdown psalm)' was a commission from the chaplaincy team at NHS Newcastle and ended up as a video, narrated by the actor Kevin Whately, to mark the birthday of the NHS in 2020. The deadline in being asked to write a poem for a person, a book or an event concentrates the mind.

'Seven blessings for a wedding' came about when my friends Sarah and George asked if I'd write a poem for their wedding, mentioning that in the collision of their family stories were at least three distinct heritages … Methodist, Jewish and no-particular-faith-at-all. It was another two friends, Holly and Joe, who asked me to write something for their big day, and that's how 'Two friends' emerged.

'Undone' was commissioned by Chine McDonald for a book to mark the 75th anniversary of Christian Aid and originally published in *Rage and Hope: 75 Prayers for a Better World* (SPCK 2021).

'Help, thanks, wow' was inspired by the writer Anne Lamott, who says in her book of the same name (published by Riverhead

Books) that these three words are the *'three essential prayers'*.

'Talking church' arrived during the 2020/21 pandemic when church doors were locked for long periods, until slowly, cautiously, people were allowed to go back inside. It first appeared in *Seeds of Hope*, a collection of daily readings published by Amos Trust.

On January 20th, 2017, in both Gambia and the USA, a new President was sworn in and the former President left: 'The four Presidents'. I was particularly interested in new President Adama Barrow because, while studying in London a few years earlier, he made ends meet as a security guard at our local Argos store on Holloway Road in North London. I like to think the President re-members my greeting him each time I prepared to leaf through the plastic catalogue pages in search of kettle or toaster.

I wrote 'A blessing for a time when the words are gone' for our friends Adrian and Judy as they lived through the final months of Adrian's life. 'Swallow' and 'Harbour' came then too, and several others, like 'The Delivery' and 'The Age of Poignant', came after his death.

Each verse of 'Hashtag Amen' was written after I'd led a funeral and composed of no more than 144 characters in the form of a single Tweet. Later Twitter increased the length to 280 characters. I didn't double the length of the verses.

I have never met anyone younger than my friend Pip Wilson, nor anyone wiser. I wrote 'Wasted' for Pip's eightieth birthday because youth has never been wasted on him.

Along with its opening scene and the 23rd Psalm, the thirteenth chapter of a letter that Paul of Tarsus wrote to the first followers of Jesus in Corinth is among the most familiar of Bible passages. Sometimes over-familiar. 'Love remix' attempts to remix love.

I have spent my life remixing love with my painter partner Meg, one of whose pieces is on the cover of this book. Meg is happiest in the garden, standing before an easel, with her children, friends … or chickens. Her happiness has a distinctive 'humming' sound.

I have used the phrase 'hit us like a truck' in 'Dear Life' in order not to use a phrase ending in a different word with the same rhyme, which I generally use when reading this poem.

The cover image of the book might appear a little grainy. It's from a low-res file of one of Meg's artworks from twenty years ago, her 'tea-bag period'. Part of a triptych of three teabags which hangs on our kitchen wall above the kettle. Whenever I walked past I thought of how much it suggests an image of Earth from space. The thought that led to it making the cover. (Visit megwroe.com)

Thanks also to my editor Neil Paynter at Wild Goose Publications for inviting me to pull this collection together while both improving my punctuation and tolerating my punctuality.

'I am the late Martin Wroe.
On the upside,
From my point of view,
I am still alive.
On the downside
You may be waiting for me.
I am late.'

Martin Wroe

@martinwroe on Twitter and Medium